THE GREATEST ROMANCE EXPOSE
BASED ON KING SOLOMON'S
ANCIENT DIARIES

THE GREATEST ROMANCE EXPOSE BASED ON KING SOLOMON'S ANCIENT DIARIES

A premarital and Marriage counseling Manual

Apostle Billy R. Woodard

authorHOUSE®

AuthorHouse™
1663 Liberty Drive
Bloomington, IN 47403
www.authorhouse.com
Phone: 1-800-839-8640

First published by AuthorHouse   08/16/2011

ISBN: 978-1-4634-8745-4 (sc)
ISBN: 978-1-4634-8744-7 (ebk)

Printed in the United States of America

Song of Solomon 1

1 The song of songs, which is Solomon's.
2 Let him kiss me with the kisses of his mouth: for thy love is better than wine.
3 Because of the savour of thy good ointments thy name is as ointment poured forth, therefore do the virgins love thee.
4 Draw me, we will run after thee: the king hath brought me into his chambers: we will be glad and rejoice in thee, we will remember thy love more than wine: the upright love thee.
5 I am black, but comely, O ye daughters of Jerusalem, as the tents of Kedar, as the curtains of Solomon.
6 Look not upon me, because I am black, because the sun hath looked upon me: my mother's children were angry with me; they made me the keeper of the vineyards; but mine own vineyard have I not kept.
7 Tell me, O thou whom my soul loveth, where thou feedest, where thou makest thy flock to rest at noon: for why should I be as one that turneth aside by the flocks of thy companions?
8 If thou know not, O thou fairest among women, go thy way forth by the footsteps of the flock, and feed thy kids beside the shepherds' tents.
9 I have compared thee, O my love, to a company of horses in Pharaoh's chariots.

10 *Thy cheeks are comely with rows of jewels, thy neck with chains of gold.*

11 *We will make thee borders of gold with studs of silver.*

12 *While the king sitteth at his table, my spikenard sendeth forth the smell thereof.*

13 *A bundle of myrrh is my well-beloved unto me; he shall lie all night betwixt my breasts.*

14 *My beloved is unto me as a cluster of camphire in the vineyards of Engedi.*

15 *Behold, thou art fair, my love; behold, thou art fair; thou hast doves' eyes.*

16 *Behold, thou art fair, my beloved, yea, pleasant: also our bed is green.*

17 *The beams of our house are cedar, and our rafters of fir.*

Song of Solomon 2

1 I am the rose of Sharon, and the lily of the valleys.
2 As the lily among thorns, so is my love among the daughters.
3 As the apple tree among the trees of the wood, so is my beloved among the sons. I sat down under his shadow with great delight, and his fruit was sweet to my taste.
4 He brought me to the banqueting house, and his banner over me was love.
5 Stay me with flagons, comfort me with apples: for I am sick of love.
6 His left hand is under my head, and his right hand doth embrace me.
7 I charge you, O ye daughters of Jerusalem, by the roes, and by the hinds of the field, that ye stir not up, nor awake my love, till he please.
8 The voice of my beloved! behold, he cometh leaping upon the mountains, skipping upon the hills.
9 My beloved is like a roe or a young hart: behold, he standeth behind our wall, he looketh forth at the windows, shewing himself through the lattice.
10 My beloved spake, and said unto me, Rise up, my love, my fair one, and come away.
11 For, lo, the winter is past, the rain is over and gone;

12 The flowers appear on the earth; the time of the singing of birds is come, and the voice of the turtle is heard in our land; 13 The fig tree putteth forth her green figs, and the vines with the tender grape give a good smell. Arise, my love, my fair one, and come away.

14 O my dove, that art in the clefts of the rock, in the secret places of the stairs, let me see thy countenance, let me hear thy voice; for sweet is thy voice, and thy countenance is comely.

15 Take us the foxes, the little foxes, that spoil the vines: for our vines have tender grapes.

16 My beloved is mine, and I am his: he feedeth among the lilies.

17 Until the day break, and the shadows flee away, turn, my beloved, and be thou like a roe or a young hart upon the mountains of Bether.

Song of Solomon 3

1 By night on my bed I sought him whom my soul loveth: I sought him, but I found him not.
2 I will rise now, and go about the city in the streets, and in the broad ways I will seek him whom my soul loveth: I sought him, but I found him not.
3 The watchmen that go about the city found me: to whom I said, Saw ye him whom my soul loveth?
4 It was but a little that I passed from them, but I found him whom my soul loveth: I held him, and would not let him go, until I had brought him into my mother's house, and into the chamber of her that conceived me.
5 I charge you, O ye daughters of Jerusalem, by the roes, and by the hinds of the field, that ye stir not up, nor awake my love, till he please.
6 Who is this that cometh out of the wilderness like pillars of smoke, perfumed with myrrh and frankincense, with all powders of the merchant?
7 Behold his bed, which is Solomon's; threescore valiant men are about it, of the valiant of Israel.
8 They all hold swords, being expert in war: every man hath his sword upon his thigh because of fear in the night.
9 King Solomon made himself a chariot of the wood of Lebanon.

10 He made the pillars thereof of silver, the bottom thereof of gold, the covering of it of purple, the midst thereof being paved with love, for the daughters of Jerusalem.
11 Go forth, O ye daughters of Zion, and behold king Solomon with the crown wherewith his mother crowned him in the day of his espousals, and in the day of the gladness of his heart.

Song of Solomon 4

1 Behold, thou art fair, my love; behold, thou art fair; thou hast doves' eyes within thy locks: thy hair is as a flock of goats, that appear from mount Gilead.
2 Thy teeth are like a flock of sheep that are even shorn, which came up from the washing; whereof every one bear twins, and none is barren among them.
3 Thy lips are like a thread of scarlet, and thy speech is comely: thy temples are like a piece of a pomegranate within thy locks.
4 Thy neck is like the tower of David builded for an armoury, whereon there hang a thousand bucklers, all shields of mighty men.
5 Thy two breasts are like two young roes that are twins, which feed among the lilies.
6 Until the day break, and the shadows flee away, I will get me to the mountain of myrrh, and to the hill of frankincense.
7 Thou art all fair, my love; there is no spot in thee.
8 Come with me from Lebanon, my spouse, with me from Lebanon: look from the top of Amana, from the top of Shenir and Hermon, from the lions' dens, from the mountains of the leopards.

9 Thou hast ravished my heart, my sister, my spouse; thou hast ravished my heart with one of thine eyes, with one chain of thy neck.

10 How fair is thy love, my sister, my spouse! how much better is thy love than wine! and the smell of thine ointments than all spices!

11 Thy lips, O my spouse, drop as the honeycomb: honey and milk are under thy tongue; and the smell of thy garments is like the smell of Lebanon.

12 A garden inclosed is my sister, my spouse; a spring shut up, a fountain sealed.

13 Thy plants are an orchard of pomegranates, with pleasant fruits; camphire, with spikenard,

14 Spikenard and saffron; calamus and cinnamon, with all trees of frankincense; myrrh and aloes, with all the chief spices:

15 A fountain of gardens, a well of living waters, and streams from Lebanon.

16 Awake, O north wind; and come, thou south; blow upon my garden, that the spices thereof may flow out. Let my beloved come into his garden, and eat his pleasant fruits.

Song of Solomon 5

1 I am come into my garden, my sister, my spouse: I have gathered my myrrh with my spice; I have eaten my honeycomb with my honey; I have drunk my wine with my milk: eat, O friends; drink, yea, drink abundantly, O beloved.
2 I sleep, but my heart waketh: it is the voice of my beloved that knocketh, saying, Open to me, my sister, my love, my dove, my undefiled: for my head is filled with dew, and my locks with the drops of the night.
3 I have put off my coat; how shall I put it on? I have washed my feet; how shall I defile them?
4 My beloved put in his hand by the hole of the door, and my bowels were moved for him.
5 I rose up to open to my beloved; and my hands dropped with myrrh, and my fingers with sweet smelling myrrh, upon the handles of the lock.
6 I opened to my beloved; but my beloved had withdrawn himself, and was gone: my soul failed when he spake: I sought him, but I could not find him; I called him, but he gave me no answer.
7 The watchmen that went about the city found me, they smote me, they wounded me; the keepers of the walls took away my veil from me.

8 I charge you, O daughters of Jerusalem, if ye find my beloved, that ye tell him, that I am sick of love.
9 What is thy beloved more than another beloved, O thou fairest among women? what is thy beloved more than another beloved, that thou dost so charge us?
10 My beloved is white and ruddy, the chiefest among ten thousand.
11 His head is as the most fine gold, his locks are bushy, and black as a raven.
12 His eyes are as the eyes of doves by the rivers of waters, washed with milk, and fitly set.
13 His cheeks are as a bed of spices, as sweet flowers: his lips like lilies, dropping sweet smelling myrrh.
14 His hands are as gold rings set with the beryl: his belly is as bright ivory overlaid with sapphires.
15 His legs are as pillars of marble, set upon sockets of fine gold: his countenance is as Lebanon, excellent as the cedars.
16 His mouth is most sweet: yea, he is altogether lovely. This is my beloved, and this is my friend, O daughters of Jerusalem.

Song of Solomon 6

1 Whither is thy beloved gone, O thou fairest among women? whither is thy beloved turned aside? that we may seek him with thee.

2 My beloved is gone down into his garden, to the beds of spices, to feed in the gardens, and to gather lilies.

3 I am my beloved's, and my beloved is mine: he feedeth among the lilies.

4 Thou art beautiful, O my love, as Tirzah, comely as Jerusalem, terrible as an army with banners.

5 Turn away thine eyes from me, for they have overcome me: thy hair is as a flock of goats that appear from Gilead.

6 Thy teeth are as a flock of sheep which go up from the washing, whereof every one beareth twins, and there is not one barren among them.

7 As a piece of a pomegranate are thy temples within thy locks.

8 There are threescore queens, and fourscore concubines, and virgins without number.

9 My dove, my undefiled is but one; she is the only one of her mother, she is the choice one of her that bare her. The daughters saw her, and blessed her; yea, the queens and the concubines, and they praised her.

10 Who is she that looketh forth as the morning, fair as the moon, clear as the sun, and terrible as an army with banners?
11 I went down into the garden of nuts to see the fruits of the valley, and to see whether the vine flourished and the pomegranates budded.
12 Or ever I was aware, my soul made me like the chariots of Amminadib.
13 Return, return, O Shulamite; return, return, that we may look upon thee. What will ye see in the Shulamite? As it were the company of two armies.

Song of Solomon 7

1 How beautiful are thy feet with shoes, O prince's daughter! the joints of thy thighs are like jewels, the work of the hands of a cunning workman.
2 Thy navel is like a round goblet, which wanteth not liquor: thy belly is like an heap of wheat set about with lilies.
3 Thy two breasts are like two young roes that are twins.
4 Thy neck is as a tower of ivory; thine eyes like the fishpools in Heshbon, by the gate of Bathrabbim: thy nose is as the tower of Lebanon which looketh toward Damascus.
5 Thine head upon thee is like Carmel, and the hair of thine head like purple; the king is held in the galleries.
6 How fair and how pleasant art thou, O love, for delights!
7 This thy stature is like to a palm tree, and thy breasts to clusters of grapes.
8 I said, I will go up to the palm tree, I will take hold of the boughs thereof: now also thy breasts shall be as clusters of the vine, and the smell of thy nose like apples;
9 And the roof of thy mouth like the best wine for my beloved, that goeth down sweetly, causing the lips of those that are asleep to speak.
10 I am my beloved's, and his desire is toward me.
11 Come, my beloved, let us go forth into the field; let us lodge in the villages.

12 Let us get up early to the vineyards; let us see if the vine flourish, whether the tender grape appear, and the pomegranates bud forth: there will I give thee my loves.
13 The mandrakes give a smell, and at our gates are all manner of pleasant fruits, new and old, which I have laid up for thee, O my beloved.

Song of Solomon 8

1 O that thou wert as my brother, that sucked the breasts of my mother! when I should find thee without, I would kiss thee; yea, I should not be despised.

2 I would lead thee, and bring thee into my mother's house, who would instruct me: I would cause thee to drink of spiced wine of the juice of my pomegranate.

3 His left hand should be under my head, and his right hand should embrace me.

4 I charge you, O daughters of Jerusalem, that ye stir not up, nor awake my love, until he please.

5 Who is this that cometh up from the wilderness, leaning upon her beloved? I raised thee up under the apple tree: there thy mother brought thee forth: there she brought thee forth that bare thee.

6 Set me as a seal upon thine heart, as a seal upon thine arm: for love is strong as death; jealousy is cruel as the grave: the coals thereof are coals of fire, which hath a most vehement flame.

7 Many waters cannot quench love, neither can the floods drown it: if a man would give all the substance of his house for love, it would utterly be contemned.

8 We have a little sister, and she hath no breasts: what shall we do for our sister in the day when she shall be spoken for?

9 If she be a wall, we will build upon her a palace of silver: and if she be a door, we will inclose her with boards of cedar.

10 I am a wall, and my breasts like towers: then was I in his eyes as one that found favour.

11 Solomon had a vineyard at Baalhamon; he let out the vineyard unto keepers; every one for the fruit thereof was to bring a thousand pieces of silver.

12 My vineyard, which is mine, is before me: thou, O Solomon, must have a thousand, and those that keep the fruit thereof two hundred.

13 Thou that dwellest in the gardens, the companions hearken to thy voice: cause me to hear it.

14 Make haste, my beloved, and be thou like to a roe or to a young hart upon the mountains of spices.

The Greatest Romance Expose (Based on King Solomons' Song Of Songs)

Pre-marital/Marriage Consultation Manual
Introduction

The literary contents in this manual does not claim absolution. The facts do agree with King Solomon's concept of relationships and romance. First King Solomon personifies the love relationship between the eternal God of heaven and His chosen people Isreal. The equal concept is set forth in King Solomon's covenant relationship with the Shulamite woman.

King Solomon in his infinite wisdom employs the symbolism of the vineyard and its fruit as expressions of the male and female nature.Apples,grapes,and passion fruit are intergrated and interchangeably employed as male and female passions, as well as anatomical human feautures. The flavor of King Solomon's wisdom is nothing short of genius and complete command of the english language.

In the archives of this manual the male will discover his <u>purpose</u> and his <u>assignment</u> in relationship to his female counterpart.It vital in our society that the male rediscover his <u>purpose </u>not only in his relationships but in this world that God created for him . . . understanding his <u>purpose</u> he can fulfill his obligation to his creator.

The male must understand that he is an expression of a God of love.We live in a society where men do not know their <u>purpose</u> or <u>assignment</u> . . . Its a small wonder why men become abusers of their female counter parts . . .they have no <u>purpose</u> or <u>assignment</u> for themselves . . . and are void of the ability to care for the females in their lives. Perhaps this manual will give birth to volume two prompting the female counterpart to her <u>purpose </u>and <u>assignment.</u>

The Shulamite woman in this epic love song mirrors every woman in our society who has suffered at the hands of fate . . . perhaps a relationship gone bad, or a family ordeal. The Shulamite woman driven from her home by sibling rivalry is forced to work the vineyards of King Solomon.The Shulamite woman seeks refuge in the vineyard fields. She finds it in a great man of valor,<u>purpose </u>and <u>assignment </u>in the person of the wise King Solomon.

King Solomon in this love song is the ancient paradigmn for the todays modern male.King Solomon represents strength,character,fortitude,and most of all the love that heals all wounds, and redeems.

My sincere prayer is that the eyes of understanding will be opened to the reader whether male or female.I pray that couples single and married will read it together . . . I pray that women and men will teach their children from this manual.

I Pray that the God of heaven will reveal through this work his eternal plan of the ages for his crown creation humanity in the earth.

God is a God of purpose . . . He had a purpose for placing man on planet earth. "The heaven,even the heavens, belong to God,but the earth he has given to the children of men". (Psalms 115:16)

"Many are the plans of a man's heart,but it is the purpose of the Lord that prevails" . . . Holy Scriptures

Chapter One

Covenant Relationship and Marriage

"Love" is the key word in the song of Solomon.Love allows the expression of desire and passion between a male and female.

Love should always be the basis for relationship and marriage.

The song of Solomon is the greatest of all songs.It is a literary work of art as well as a theological masterpiece. The song was given to Isreal,God's chosen.The song itself is like the sumptuous fruit it personifies, alive with color and full of seeds. Quite unlike any other biblical book it merits special consideration as a biblical archtype.

<u>The Covenant Marriage</u>

And the Lord God said, "It is not good that man should be alone;I will make him an help meet for him". Genesis 2:18 (KJV).

The male and the female are the object of God's eternal love.The male and the female are empowered to express and share love resulting in a utopia of romance,case in point,King Solomon and the Shulamite woman.

Understand something,God did not create a help meet equal to Adam (another man),but a woman to compliment and complete his exsistence. The two together would manifest the mystery of godliness,the two would become one.

The Undefiled Bed

> Marriage is honourable in all,and the bed is undefiled . . . Heb.13:4 (KJV)

The above passage of scripture in question does not convey the idea that romance can only take place in the bedroom,but has a much more profound concept.The consumation of marriage through sexual intercourse is a physical sign of a spiritual act . . . remember the mystery of godliness mention earlier . . .the two become one? Consumation through sexual intercourse creates a bond between two spirits making them one flesh. Perhaps this explains the fact that when a male and female engage in premarital intercourse,long after the relationship has dissolved the emotional bond remains intact.Understand something, marriage consumated through sexual intercourse takes on a high vow of concecration . . . What God hath joined together,let no man put asunder.

The Power Of The Undefiled Bed

I have decked my bed with coverings of tapestry,with carved woods,with fine linen from Egypt.I haved perfumed my bed with myrrh,aloes,and cinnamon,come let us take our fill of love until the morning;let us solace ourselves with love.Prov.7:16-18 (KJV)

The beauty of the undefiled bed accentuate romance via the senses . . . the spark ignites the flame to romance . . .

Chapter Two

I Come To The Garden

> Let him kiss me with the kisses of his
> mouth;for thy love is better than wine . . .
> Song Of Solomon 1:2 (KJV).

King Solomon's epic expose begins with the (loved) the shulamite woman seeking the (beloved) King Solomon for his affection.

The female in the covenant relationship (marriage) not only desires affection but requires it.The primary need of the female in the relationship is affection.The male in the relationship thinks that it is a "no brainer" that the female initially desires him sexually,understand something sex is only the experience.

The pinnacle of need for the female is affection in the relationship.The primary need of the male in the relationship is fulfillment. In the relationship the fulfillment of of both parties is the catalyst to a romance never to be forgotten as you will witness with King Solomon and the shulamite woman.

The Thought Process

The neurological composition of the male and female are considerably different. The male naturally is a "logical thinker" He becomes emotional later on in the process. The female is a "emotional thinker"often what she says is what she feels and does as opposed to what she thinks so there must be a meeting of minds between both parties. In the above scriptural verse the shulamite woman enters the garden seeking her (beloved) King Solomon for his affection.King Solomon adores his (loved one) the shulamite woman questing for fulfillment . . .

The females' first reaction will be an "emotional" one.The males first reaction will be a "logical" one.The male thinks in a straight line,the distance between two points which enables him to see the goal (vision) and to focus his energies on reaching the goal in a staight forward and direct way. The male says what he thinks. The female say what she feels.The male must understand and consider the emotional status of his help meet which defines who she is and validates her values . . . Sometime just a telephone call,a dozen roses,or maybe a warm embrace will satisfy her need for affection.

The males neurological process allows him to think in a grid . . . a straight line . . . the female neurological process allows her to perceive in more detail than the male.The female can see the whole picture and allows her to multitask in her thinking, her actions,and all that she does.Once both neurological patterns are understood and the demands are met a combustible romantic interlude ensues,much like that of King Solomon and the shulamite woman.

!WARNING!

The literary syntax in the ensueing chapters will intensify and will require the adult mind and imagination to come into full capacity. This manual is not an attempt to satisfy the carnal mind or the fleshly lust,but to set forth the naked truth concerning the covenant relationship (marriage) as God has ordained it to be.

Chapter Three

The Language Of Mutual Love

> While the king sitteth at his table,my
> spikenard sendeth forth the smell thereof;a
> bundle of myrrh is my well beloved
> (Solomon) unto me,he shall lie all night
> betwixt my breast . . .
> Song Of Solomon 1:12-13 (KJV).

As the corresponding needs of the covenant partners are met the language of love transliterates into songs of romance.The lover sings of her beloved,and he of she . . . She sings of his kingly allure as the calming essence of myrrh intermingled with her passion as spikenard creating an ambiance bonding the two together as one. Fettered together, her to him,He to her . . . He is drawn to her breast as a new born.

He lies betwixt her breast. The cleavage of her well defined breast affords a place of refuge for him to rest his head . . . As he reposes betwixt her breast his ear picks up the rhythm of her heart beat it is the beginning of a symphony . . . It is the prelude to a masterpiece.

The cleavage of her breast becomes a conclave to his male sensory mechanism . . . his heartbeat connects with hers the composition is ingenious. As he lies betwixt her breast the foundation of the greatest romance expose is laid . . .

My beloved is unto me as a cluster of camphire in the vineyard of Engedi. Song Of Solomon 1:14 (KJV).

The lover sings of her experience with her beloved as the essence of Henna (cluster of flowers) of Engedi (geographical setting in the middle east that produces the henna cluster with its calming aroma).

The Eyes Of Romance

Behold,thou art fair,my love;behold,thou art
fair;thou hast doves eyes . . . Song Of
Solomon 1:15 (KJV).

In the first stages of the romance the covenant partners critique each other through the eyes of love. He,the beloved envisions her as fair and posessing the eyes of doves the purest Of God's creation in the animal kingdom . . .the very epitome of God's Holy Spirit . . . Earlier in this chapter she the loved envisioned him,the beloved as a bundle of myrrh . . . the sweet smelling savor to her soul . . .

In chapter four the interlude continues breaking forth with virile imagery . . . robust flavor . . . intense symbolism . . . the seemingly graphic vernacular is the spice of every marriage culminating in the greatest romance expose this side of heaven.

Chapter four in entitled "His Banner Over Me Is Love" . . .

King Solomon metaphorically uses the richness,the colorfulness,the freshness of the fruit in his vineyard as expressions of the passionate human spirit as well as the anatomical feautures of the human body . . .!Get Ready . . .Read!

Chapter Four

His Banner Over Me Is Love

As the apple tree among the trees of the wood so is my beloved among the sons,I sat down under his shadow with great delight,and his fruit was sweet to my taste.He brought me to the banqueting house and his banner over me was love.Stay with me flagons comfort me with apples,for Iam sick with love . . . His left hand is under my head,and his right hand does embrace me

Song Of Solomon 2:3-6

Your banner over me is love.You are majestic,so desireous.I bow in your shadow with expectant submission.The fruit of your loin hang so perfectly in its place . . . You are appealing to my eyes and sweet to my imagination. I draw close. I breathe on you as a gentle east breeze. Your majestic maleness is intoxicating. I feel your left hand beneath my head and your right hand embrace my body.I open myself to you.I feel you penetrate my passion while tameing my unbridled spirit. I sense your movements are precise like a swiss timepiece.your slow gentle thrusts are pure ecstacy like I have never known. As you seek your pleasure while pleasing me the rhythm of my heart pulsates with your body while my emotions spin out of control. Your body is rigid,your breatheing is intense.Suddenly I feel your release,finallyI taste your majesty sweet . . . I look into your eyes and tell you I love you and declare that your banner over me is love.

Chapter Five

The Ultimate Marriage Consumation

> Awake,O north wind;and come thou south;
> blow upon my garden,that the spices thereof
> may flow out.Let my beloved come into his
> garden and eat his pleasant fruits . . .Song Of
> Solomon 4:16

My beloved you are as the cold north wind and the soft south breeze. I pray thee come blow upon my garden entreating its spices to flow in abundance for you in whom my soul delights.My beloved you are the pinnacle of my desire. You sit on the throne of my emotions,my passions,and my longings. My beloved I delight in your touch,your majesty,just the glance of your affection. Come into my garden eat your pleasure to its fullest so that we who are consumed may be consumated for it is our vow of higher concecration . . .

My beloved I was created for your purpose,your pleasure,and your passion.My spices,aloes,cinnamons,and spikenard are gathered for your pleasure . . . I lie upon my night bed alseep,but my heart is awake for you . . . beloved come into my garden cultivate its ground,plant your seed,reap your harvest. I will not keep myself from you except for our season. Beloved come into the banqueting house as did I,for it is a festival,the feast of romance.

Chapter Six

Sex vs Consumation

Marriage is honourable in all,and the bed is
undefiled;but whoremongers and adulterers
God will judge.

Hebrews 13:4 (KJV).

The new age society has coined two phrases in an effort
to define sex . . . synonomous phrases such as "making
love,"sleeping together" neither of which are correct.
Pre-marital sex is the physical act without the spiritual
attachment.Ignorance has taken the physical act of sex
to the repulsive level of perversion.

Webster's dictionary defines sex as intercourse with
persons of the opposite gender having different sexual
organs . . . sex with animals . . . same sex partners . . . is
not sex, but perversion in every sense of the word. It is
the misuse and abuse of the physical act.

In chapter one we established the fact that God
did not create Adams help meet (another man) but his

opposite . . .woman who would complete everthing that God had begun in him.

In the intro of this manual we touched on the male <u>assignment</u> and <u>purpose</u> as an expression of the eternal God of love . . . Ignorance of his <u>purpose</u> and <u>assignment</u> and God's will for his life, man has ventured onto all these avenues we have mentioned in this manual . . .The moment humanity understands its <u>assignment</u> and <u>purpose</u> . . . It will align them with the Kingdom of God and His righteousness.

The Male Purpose

Understand something,<u>purpose</u> is a plan through a process with a determined expected end. The God of heaven is a God of <u>purpose</u>. God works according to His <u>purpose</u>. The work of God has to do with the kingdom. God created spirit man for His <u>purpose</u>,therefore man is a kingdom entity.Man is a creature of dominion. Man seperated from his <u>purpose</u> will self-destruct.

The <u>purpose</u> of a product determines its design,its nature,and its feautures. <u>Purpose</u> defines the males' priorities,position,and <u>assignment</u>.

The Male Priority

The ordinal creation of man does not connotate his value but his <u>purpose</u> which aligns him with his priority . . . Understand and I reiterate man was not created first because he was more important than the woman . . . man was designed to be a creature of priority . . . If man is not busy with his <u>assignment</u>,then he does not have priority and he has no business doing anything else.

The male <u>assignment</u> with priority is the foundation upon which society is built. The home,the church,the communities are crying out for the male model and his <u>assignment</u> with his priority.

<u>The Male Assignment</u>

The male <u>purpose</u> is always defined by his <u>assignment</u>. The male <u>assignment</u> defines mans <u>purpose</u> then aligns him with his priorities.Jesus Christ understood this concept even as a child.

> How is it that ye sought me . . . wist ye not
> that I must be about my fathers' business? . . .
> Luke 2:49 (KJV).

The man was given <u>assignment</u> and dominion.This does not suggest that the woman cannot have dominion or vision . . .she had not been extracted from man as of yet . . .she would complete that which he was lacking after all she was the rib taken from his side.

The male <u>assignment</u> answeres the the ancient question raised by the wise king David . . ." Lord what is man that thou taketh knowledge of him or the son of man that thou taketh account of him? . . . It took the son of man to redeem the fallen created man to bring him back to <u>assignment,purpose</u>, and position.

The male alone must take his responsibility serious without his <u>assignment,purpose,</u>and his position . . .all the important things are lost . . . God gave Adam dominion over ever living creature . . . Adam was the first earthly king . . . The first thing Adam was given was a kingdom to rule . . . the lost of that kingdom resulted in the loss of all things spiritual,physical,and emotional.

Chapter Seven

The Lost Art Of Romance

> By Night on my bed I sought him whom my
> soul loveth;but I found him not. Song Of
> Solomon 3:1 (King James Version)

Romance is an art that is expressed with the paint brush of <u>purpose</u> on the canvass of covenant relationship (marriage).Unfortunately the art of romance has been lost or obscured via the vehicles of cultural ignorance and confusion.

The romance set forth in King Solomon's diary is not one of mechanical design but of <u>purpose.</u> The romance in the Song of Solomon chronicles the love of The eternal God of heaven for His creation. The same love is expressed with intensity and intimacy in the King Solomon diaries resulting in a utopian romance between King Solomon and the Shulamite woman.The immortal love of God prompted the creation of man in God's own image and after his likeness . . . making man the exact expression of that same immortal love.

In the covenant relationship (marriage) the female counterpart is an extension and expression of man,therefore bearing the same potential to express and share that same immortal love,after all she is Adams's rib.

If the covenant relationship (marriage) is to experience the romance set forth in Solomon's diary,it must not be duplicated but experienced via male and female <u>purpose</u>

<u>Violation Of Purpose and Assignment</u>

The ignorance of <u>purpose</u> and <u>assignment</u> has progenated a dysfunctional society of degenerates.The misinterpretation of love has been the compass that has directed humanity away from the love of God onto the path of the false concept of love of the god of this world (satan).

The hope of our society lies in the rediscovery of its <u>purpose</u> and its <u>assignment.</u>

> I will arise now,and go about the city and
> the streets,and in the broken ways I will seek
> him whom my soul loveth . . .
> **Song Of Solomon 3:2**

Humanity must understand that Christ is the paradigmn for its <u>purpose</u> and <u>assignment.</u> Christ came to redeem and realign mankind with God's will and <u>purpose</u> for their lives.

Our world must search relentlessly to find its way back to God.Estrangement from God alienates every aspect of our lives leaving us vulnerable to the wiles of the god of this world (satan).

The rediscovery of God's love through <u>purpose</u> and <u>assignment</u> will once again help us in experiencing God's best in every area of our lives from worship to relationship . . .

Chapter Eight

Rediscovery-A Show Of Affection

Thy neck is like the tower of David . . .
Song of Solomon 4:4

The rediscovery of the male and female <u>purpose</u> and <u>assignment</u> takes the covenant relationship to the next dimension.King Solomon expresses his heartfelt passion to the Shulamite woman . . .

The beloved (Solomon) makes a show of affection. He rustles the trace hair along her neckline with the wind of his breath.He gently kisses and breathes on her from the crown of her head to the nape of her neck.He overlays the windblown path with the kisses of his mouth,minutes seem like hours as he pursues her response. The beloved King Solomon is passionate,skillful like an artisan at his craft. The moisture of his kisses mingled with the layers of aloes,myrrh,and cinnamon on her body creates a pervasive chemistry very suttle but powerful.

The silhoutte of her neckline personifies King David's tower stern,and erect. King Solomon descends the tower like a silver fox dismounting into the underbrush of her passion.King Solomon is gentle and majestic in his pursuit,his conquest is intoxicating.

The Shulamite woman is entangled in his web of affection.The needs of both parties are met . . . in this emotional conquest . . .

A season of ecstacy will ensue . . . his show of affection is the catalyst for a budding romance.

Thy breasts are like two young roes that are twins,which feed among the lillies . . . Song of Solomon 4:5

Kings Solomon's show of affection intensifies as he epitomizes her breast as two new born fawns . . . youthful,developed,supple to the touch.King Solomon imagines her breasts as twin roes feeding on her beauty.

King Solomon's speech is that of a master orator,yet he capitalizes on the Shulamite woman's beauty . . . Your eyes are like doves eyes,your lips are like threads of scarlet . . . King Solomon concedes "Thou hast ravished my heart,my sister,my spouse,thou hast ravished my heart . . . note the profound fulfillment of the Shulamite woman as a sister,a spouse,and a help meet.

King Solomon understands his <u>purpose </u>and <u>assignment</u> to the Shulamite woman,therefore he recognizes her God given <u>purpose </u>and <u>assignment</u> to his life . . . not just as a female but an integral part of him that has been missing . . . since God awakened him from the deep sleep . . ." This is bone of my bone,and flesh of my flesh" . . . thou shalt be called woman.

Chapter Nine

The Male Purpose (continued)

In chapter six we defined purpose as it relates to the male species as a plan through a process with a expected and determined end.God created man with a purpose and therefore man's end is determined by a God of purpose. Note God's decree given to Moses for the children of Isreal" And ye shall be unto me a kingdom of preists;and an holy nation,these are the words which thou shall speak unto the children of Isreal" (KJV).

> Man left to his own <u>purpose</u> and <u>assignment</u> will self destruct. Many are the plans of a man's heart,but its the Lord's purpose that prevails . . .Proverbs 19:21

All men in our society,myself included,have tried to contend with the varied male <u>purpose roles</u> set forth in society,only to be ensnared in a maze of utter confusion. Understand something,<u>purpose is not purpose</u> as it relates to the male species unless it comes from the throne room of heaven. It was God's will and desire to extend heavens government through mankind.

The sons of God have a mandate and that is to multiply, subdue, and replenish the earth ... take dominion. Understand something the kingdom etimology of the word "sons" does not suggest gender, but born again souls.

God created man in His image and after His likeness . . .and tabernacled him (spirit) in two houses, male and female . . .created he them . . . (Genesis 1:27).

The male purpose can be catagorized in three groupings. Priority, Position, and Assignment." These three mandates govern mankinds's very exsistence.

Priority-makes reference to mankind's order of creation. The order does not suggest his improtance over the woman, but his responsibility to all humanity.

Position-alludes to the environment he governs . . . Adam was never to leave the garden, his purpose was to extend the garden into the rest of the earth.

> Assignment-the task mankind has been given to carry out . . . mankind was to multiply, subdue, and replenish the earth from the garden environment ... Understand something, the garden was Adam's Kingdom. The first thing God gave mankind was a kingdom . . . And the Lord God planted a garden eastward in Eden; and there he put the man whom he had formed.
> Genesis 2:8

It is imperative that the male species understand his purpose in a world that God created for him.

Statistics are proof positive that the male species does not understand his role . . .consider the various venues in society.In the business sector there are two women to every man.In the religious community there are three women to every man.

Two thirds of societies women work away from the home,while three thirds of societies men are Mr. Moms . . . stay at home dads. I do not condemn these statistics but do concede that most of them are for convenience rather than necessity.

If the male species is confused concerning his priority,his position,and his assignment it stand to reason he is not clear on much of anything else.

If the male counterpart of the of the covenant relationship (marriage) understand his purpose . . . then his female counterpart can respect and acknowledge his position of authority in her life.

In chapter ten the Shulamite woman acknowledges King Solomon's kingly authority over his kingdom and his subjects,as well as the authority in her life.

It is my very strong opinion for couples considering marriage to undergo premarital counseling . . . its imperative that the males and females understand each species in the light of <u>purpose</u> and <u>assignment.</u>

The male must understand his <u>purpose</u> and <u>assignment</u> to leave his mother and his father and cleave to his wife . . . if this is true then what can be said of the man who leaves his wife and goes home to his mother and father?????????

The central focus of this manual is on the male.His ordinal creation,being created first has nothhing to do with his importance over the woman but everything to do with his responsibility to her and everthing else that

God created and gave him dominion over.As we stated in earlier documentation,perhaps this manual will ingnite the flame for volume two of "The Greatest Romance Expose" setting forth the <u>purpose</u> and <u>assignment </u>of the female in relation to her creation.

God placed man in an environment where he could carry out his <u>purpose</u> and <u>assignment</u>. God placed man in the garden of eden . . . The garden was a geographical venue equal to heaven itself.Eden comes from the hebrew word meaning "delightful", "pleasant". The word garden means "enclosed" . . . I reiterate again,Adam was never to leave the garden but was to work from within the garden . . . extending the garden into the rest of the world. The garden represented Adam always being in the presence of God.Man still has an eden that places him suprnaturally in the presence of God. Man has become eden for he himself houses the very presence of God in his temple.(1 Cor.6:19). It is of vital importance that man realizes his union with God through Jesus Christ,our king. A man without God literally has no conscience and cannot be trusted. His affinities are to the demands of the world system and the god of this world.He has little if any at all loyalty to his <u>purpose </u>and his <u>assignment.</u> "The heart is deceitful and desperately wicked and who can know it . . . ?" (Jer. 17:9).

The male in the covenant relationship (marriage) must understand that his <u>purpose </u>and his <u>assignment</u> takes high priority over his sexual conquest,yes even in his marriage.

The male <u>purpose </u>and <u>asignment </u>sets his priorities as the teacher,the cultivator,and the provider. As the teacher God has equipped the male with the information to govern his society.The male is not the teacher because he is smarter but because he was given the vital information first.The teacher is submissive to his <u>purpose</u> and <u>assignment</u> therefore submission is imparted to his environment enableing their respect to his governing authority.

As the cultivator,the male must not perform thoughtless activity.He must think things out in order to work it for the good of all concerned. Cultivate means to make something grow and produce a greater yield. The male has an awesome responsibility to all things and persons in his realm of authority that is what defines him as a king.

As the provider,the male (ladies) is not defined by his muscle and brawn.Its the work that he does that reveals his potential as a provider . . . (I do mean his work outside the bedroom ladies).

The male as a provider must make available those commodities that give quality of life to all that is under his governorship this earns him repect in every aspect of life . . .even in the bedroom.

Chapter Ten

The Male Purpose Acknowledged

Go forth O ye daughters of Zion,and behold
King Solomon with the crown wherewith his
mother crowned him . . .
Song Of Solomon 3:11

The Shulamite woman acknowledges King Solomon for his kingly statesmanship. The Shulamite woman characterizes his maleness and his <u>purpose</u> as his crown. She exhorts the daughters of zion just to behold the fair king.

In the covenant relationship it is imperative that the males's <u>purpose</u> and <u>assignment</u> be recognized and respected as his kingly qualities. The female must understand that these qualities alone he must assume. She as the helpmeet will enhance these qualities making the relationship complete.It is when the male and female <u>purpose</u> are taken for granite that the covenant relationship suffers demolition.

The Shulamite woman praises Solomon's kingship, she realizes it is his dominion and not domination which affords her the liberation to be who she was created to be. She realizes that his domain provides a safe place, a place of provision, a haven for her development of whom God has called her to be.

The Male as Visionary

The female counterpart in the covenant relationship realizes that her husband is a visionary. The visionary knows who he is and understands his <u>purpose</u> and <u>assignment.</u> The visionary does not copy the patterns and molds of society. The female understands that her husband is gifted with the birthing of vision. "Where there is no vision, the people perish" (Prov. 29:18).

The visionary knows where he is going and has detailed perception of how to get there. The visionary does not make a move and wonder what his next step will be.

The Shulamite woman accredited King Solomon's visionary ability as his crown. The Shulamite woman praised Solomon's wisdom in every situation. King Solomon had the ability to receive the vision and the wisdom to carry it out.

Understand something, the fact that the husband is the visionary does not downplay the role of the wife . . . the female often times enhances the vision for she is one with the husband and the vision is not distorted or does not become a division.

Jesus Christ in his human form realized the importance of vision . . . he had the full vision and understand of the kingom of God and so proclaimed it to Pilate and I quote "My kingdom is not of this world" ... Jesus clearly did not come to fix this broken world system,but to replace it with the vision and purpose of God's heavenly kingdom on earth ... Jesus was a man of vision.

Created/Designed for Vision

Remember,man was not created first because of his importance over woman.He was created and designed to receive,process and carry out vision according to his creator's will and desire.The woman was created to make sure man would accomplish his vision ... case in point King Solomon was the owner of the vineyard,but the Shulamite woman worked the vineyard with her hands ... she understood that Solomon has the vision and she was to help him bring it to fruition.

The Shulamite woman in our textual verse in question ... epitomizes King Solomon as wearing a crown ... could it be that she understood in her spirit that he was precursor to the King of Kings who would be adorned with the eternal crown of God and heir to the eternal kingdom ... ? It is clear that the Shulamite woman acknowledged Solomons's <u>purpose</u> and <u>assignment</u> . The Shulamite woman exhorted the daughters of Zion to behold Solomon's splendor and his crowning allure as the male factor in the covenant relationship (marriage). Suffice it to say that the male counterpart in the covenant relationship (marriage) is the covering and the crowing act of an eternal God.

After acknowledgeing King Solomons's <u>purpose,</u> the Shulamite woman decree her undying love for him.

Chapter Eleven

The Shulamite womans' Decree Of Love

"Many waters cannot quench love,neither
can the floods drown it; if a man would
give all the substance of his house for love,it
would utterly be contemned".

Song Of Solomon 8:7

The Shulamite woman decrees that the strongest currents
of the oceans of the earth cannot quench the burning
flames of love she holds for King Solomon. She futher
concedes that the vehement hurricanes of all the seas
cannot drown her passion for him . . . the very essence of
King Solomon is the air that she breathes.

In the presence of King Solomon the very essence
of the Shulamite woman is released. The walls of her
inhibition cannot withstand the pressure of her passions.
The wall are bulging with raw desire,lust,and passion
for the king.

The Shulamite womans'love for Solomon is
unbridled.

> "Make haste, my beloved, and be thou like to
> a roe or to a young hart upon the mountain
> of spices".
> Song Of Solomon 8:14

The Shulamite woman pleads with King "Inulge me my love,as a hart would a roe" I am yours and you are mine.

The hart and the roe are drawn only by their animal magnitism . . . the mountain atmosphere beckons them to a chance encounter . . . the roe knows nothing but utter submisssion to the hart . . . as does the Shulamite woman to King Solomon.

> My beloved standeth behind the wall,he
> looketh forth at the windows,shewing
> himself through the lattice.
> Song Of Solomon 2:9

The Shulamite woman eptiomizes Solomon as buck roe peering through the lattice window . . . only revealing the silhoutte of his Physique . . . she pleads with him "Until the day break,and the shadows flee away,turn, my beloved,and be thou like a buck upon the mountains" . . . She entreats Solomon to solace her with his love throuhout the night until the evening shadows fade into oblivion and the morning breaks through . . . "Iam yours,and you are mine".

The love that the Shulamite woman has found in Solomon most couples,relationships,and yes even marriages only dream of. I pray that as you continue to read and study this manual that you will understand that your relationship,your marriage can realize and experience this type of love through the vehicle of God's <u>purpose</u> and <u>assignment</u> for both of your lives.It was God's decree for Adam and Eve in the garden.It is God's decree for you in planet earth.

> **Seek ye first the Kingdom . . .**
> **Matthew 6:33**

Chapter Twelve

Utter Praise

"Thou are all fair, my love; there is no spot in thee".

Song Of Solomon 4:7

In response to the Shulamite womans' decree of love; King Solomon reciprocates with utter praise. King Solomon pesonifies the woman's locks of hair as the breath-taking beauty of the gilean goats of Lebanon . . . (Song Of Solomon 4:1) His tongue is as a torch ingniting the flames of her emotion and passions.

King Solomon is intimately descriptive. He envisons the thickness and beauty of her lips as dropped honey comb with the venon of milk and honey under her tongue.

Song Of Solomon 4:11

King Solomon's paint brush imagination sketches a comlete composite of the woman inside and out. (Read chapter four in its entirety).

King Solomon's zesty vernacular arrest the mind of his readers,setting the Shulamite woman forth as the princess of Lebanon;beholding to every eye and desirous of every Lebanese heart . . . King Solomon conclude his praise with his signature of proposal to the Shulamite woman . . ."Come with me from Lebanon,my spouse . . . (Song Of Solomon 4:8).

The Summary

If you have read the prior twelve chapters,then you have experienced first hand "The Greatest Romance Expose" based on the King Solomon diaries.

My endeavor in creating this manual is to mentally fulfill you,intellecually inform you,and spirituall charge you.

After reading King Solomon's Song Of Songs more times than I care to remember,I decided by revelation of course that Solomon can better help us understand the purpose and assignment of the human entity created a man and born a male by the sovereign will of God. The male purpose and his assignment and relationship as it relates to the world created for him and all things surrounding him is key to this interval of history.

King Solomon's song of songs is a spiritual prod to unequally yoked relationships and crumbling marriages,in that it challenges openess,growth,and happiness in the relationship as well as in the marriage culminating in a romantic expose.

King Solomon in his covenant relationship with the Shulamite woman personifies Jehovah God's covenant relationship with his chosen Isreal and Christ's covenant relationship with the church his bride. King Solomon is the endorsement to the apostle Paul's letter to the Ephesians "husbands love your wives,even as Christ loved the church and gave his life for it" (Ephesians 5:25). King Solomon undertands his paradigmn role undergirding his purpose and assignment in relationship to his female counterpart.

The male in this interval of history must be crystal clear on his purpose and assignment as it is the foundation upon which family,society,the church,and the Kingdom Of God rest.King Solomon understood the magnitude of his purpose and assignment. He went to God in prayer. "Give me now wisdom and knowledge, that I may go out and come in before this people:for who can judge this thou people,that is so great?

2 Chronicles 1:10

It would be a monument to our male society in question,if we would follow Solomon's lead in surrendering our hearts an souls to the God of heaven,allowing his judgement to become ours.

We.the king/preist unto God could then fulfill the kingdom mandate placed upon us and rule the world created for us with the dominion anointing that rest upon us and resides within us.

> "What? Know ye not that your body is
> the temple of the Holy Ghost which is in
> you,which ye have of God . . .
> 1 Corinthianns 6:19